EXMOUTH

Century – Part One

George Pridmore

With all best wishes
George Pridmore

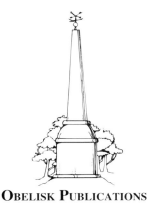

OBELISK PUBLICATIONS

ALSO BY THE AUTHOR

Wish You Were Here at Exmouth
From Exmouth With Love
From Budleigh Salterton With Love
Entertaining Exmouth
Exmouth Century – Part Two

OTHER TITLES IN THIS SERIES

Ashburton of Yesteryear, *John Germon and Pete Webb*
The Teign Valley of Yesteryear, Parts I and II, *Chips Barber*
Brixham of Yesteryear, Parts I, II and III, *Chips Barber*
Pinhoe of Yesteryear, Parts I and II, *Chips Barber*
Princetown of Yesteryear, Parts I and II, *Chips Barber*
Kingsteignton of Yesteryear, *Richard Harris*
Heavitree of Yesteryear, *Chips Barber*
Kenton and Starcross of Yesteryear, *Eric Vaughan*
Ide of Yesteryear, *Mavis Piller*

We have over 160 Devon titles; for a full list please send an SAE to
Obelisk Publications, 2 Church Hill, Pinhoe, Exeter EX4 9ER

Acknowledgements

I am very grateful to those folk who have provided photographs and information about them, and to those photographers, known and unknown, whose work may be reproduced here.

Thanks also to Chips and Sally Barber for their continued support.

First published in 2000 by
Obelisk Publications, 2 Church Hill, Pinhoe, Exeter, Devon
Designed and Typeset by Sally Barber
Printed in Great Britain

EXMOUTH

Century – Part One

At the start of the twentieth century, Exmouth could have been described as a small compact town hugging the Exe Estuary, despite the fact that it had recently been formed into an Urban District which included the villages of Withycombe and Littleham. The population then was just under 10,000.

One hundred years later that description no longer applies. The century – particularly the second half – has seen the town expand tremendously, with housing and industrial development on what was previously agricultural land. And the population has more than trebled.

This book may be described as a snapshot album of Exmouth over those one hundred years. Like most family albums, the emphasis is on people, although some events and places are included.

A number of the pictures have been featured during the past 17 years in my weekly "Peep into the Past" column in the *Exmouth and East Devon Journal*.

The horse was the major form of transport around the town in the early part of the century, as these two advertisements from 1902 for F. W. Attwater and G. Hayne & Son indicate.

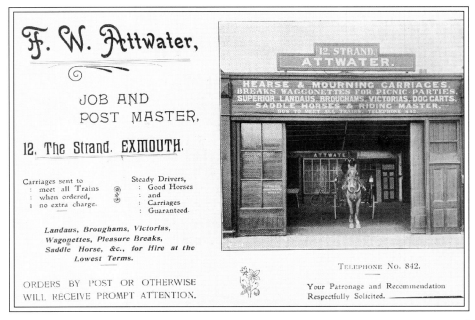

A cabby who ignored the coming of the motor car was Alf Knowles, seen here in his cab at his pick-up point outside Exmouth Railway Station. With his own one-horse power he continued to ply his trade until 1938, thus earning the title of Exmouth's last horse cab.

The business of Tucker's on The Strand was established in the town in 1801. Here's how the premises looked shortly after completing its first 100 years of trading. And with its 200th anniversary rapidly approaching, Tucker's is still in business at the same site.

(Opposite, top) Baths, broom heads, buckets, coal scuttles, mats, oil lamps and spades. These were among goods displayed for sale outside Ebdon's ironmongery shop at 15 Albion Street in the early days of the century. And a notice in the window confirms that he also sells methylated spirit at sixpence a pint.

(Below) It would seem that when local councillors carried out an inspection of the town's waterworks in 1906, they decided the best way to do so would be to take a drink of its product. At least, it is presumably water in the glasses they are holding! The Urban District Council had acquired the town's water supply from a private Water Company four years earlier.

(Bottom) Mr Salter and his pupils. In the early part of the century, the sons of many of the town's professional and

business men received their education at the private school run by Charles Salter. Situated originally at 13 Moreton Crescent, it later moved to 49 Victoria Road.

An event which stunned local residents on March 14, 1906 was the disastrous fire at Bystock House on the outskirts of the town. Ownership of the old mansion had just changed hands and, at the time of the fire, was unoccupied while alterations and conversions were being carried out. The efforts of Exmouth and Exeter fire brigades, together with those of estate employees and workmen, could not prevent the building from being virtually destroyed. Bystock House was later rebuilt and today is operated by a charity as a Sheltered Home.

This band of musicians used to help spread the Christian Gospel in Exmouth during the early part of the century. They were members of the local Salvation Army, a body which is still active in the town, but without a band these days.

There was great excitement in October 1907 when the Russian schooner *Tehwija* was wrecked off Orcombe Point, and its cargo of timber, along with wreckage from the ship, was strewn along the beach. All nine crew members were saved and taken to the Sailors' Rest, which then stood on Chapel Hill. Three months later foundation stones were laid for

a new Sailors' Rest in St Andrews Road. A list of subscriptions towards the cost showed one from "His Excellency the Russian Ambassador", presumably prompted by the *Tehwija* incident.

THE

NEW SAILORS' REST

St. Andrew's Road, Exmouth.

THE

Laying of the Foundation Stones

*The Most Hon. the Marquis of Ailsbury
and the Hon. Sec. (Mrs. B. Anderson).*

Took place on Saturday, Jan. 18th, 1908.

Dressed as Swiss Misses, and ready to do duty as stall holders at a three-day Swiss Bazaar in the Public Hall in February 1911, were Mrs Sharman, Miss Heal, Rosie Croft, Amy Law, Nellie Walters, Miss Law, Laura Dodd, Nellie Smith, Violet Greenaway and Nellie Mortimore.

A number of today's soccer clubs had their roots in places of worship. In the early days of the game it was not uncommon for a church or church organisation to have its own football team. The eleven players seen here, together with a clergyman, were members of Exmouth Church Institute AFC during the 1917/18 season. The cleric was the Rev Howard Frayling, one of four curates at Holy Trinity Church at the time. The team comprised local lads Monty Carter, Harold Letten, Percy Holman, Jim Southwell, Bill Knott, Percy Nicholl, Jim Salter, C. Perriam, "Crongy" Nicholl and Albert Pratte, plus a "foreigner" – from Lympstone!

The local Young Men's Christian Association also had its own soccer club, as pictured here in the 1920/21 season.

It was netball time when the photographer visited Exeter Road School sometime in the early 1920s.

Throughout the century, the Starcross Ferry has maintained a link with the other side of the Exe Estuary, originally operating all year round but in later years only in the summer. Although vessels providing the service had various names, the one launched in 1923 was actually called *Starcross*. Her first skipper was G. Prowse.

Sunny South Devon

COME TO EXMOUTH

PASSENGER TO EXMOUTH.

W. J. Delderfield & Sons, Printers, Exmouth.

(Above) A typical packed beach scene in the 1920s. There are buckets and spades, but not a swim suit or bathing costume in sight. And everyone is wearing headgear of some kind.

(Left) A poster printed by W. J. Delderfield & Sons, with an invitation to spend a holiday in Exmouth sometime during the late 1920s/early 1930s. William J. Delderfield came to Devon from London in 1923 to take over the *Exmouth Chronicle* newspaper. He was later succeeded as editor first by his son E. R. (Eric), who was later to write many West Country books, and then his other son R. F. (Ron), who went on to become an author and playwright of international repute.

(Opposite, top) Although traffic wardens as we know them today did not appear on our streets until the 1960s, Exmouth had one around 40 years earlier. William Alexander is on traffic control duty outside the London Hotel at the busy junction of Exeter Road, Albion Street, Chapel Street and The Parade in 1928. That was the year in which the Devon Joint Standing

Committee introduced a scheme of what it called traffic controllers, but were actually referred to in Press reports as traffic wardens.

(Below) A group of mothers line up with their babies in the mid-1920s. The occasion was a Baby Show in Phear Park. Note the fashionable hats of the mums.

The town's cricket club has a history dating back to 1860. These members (circa 1925) were named as: Maden, G. Jennings, A. R. Hall, G. A. W. Monk, W. G. Blackwell, Sanders, Capt F. J. C. Hunter, F. H. Carroll, Major D. C. Greenlees, Capt C. R. L. Aspinall, H. S. Carter, Cockgrave, J. J. Jefferies, L. P. Sweet and N. Ford.

In the picture below it is 1928 and a flying boat is moored in the Exe Estuary, with the Pier Pavilion in the background. This was one of two such aircraft in the area for most of the summer that year. They were said to be involved in a proposal to construct a barrage across the Estuary from the Warren to the Dock area. The idea was to provide both a flying-boat base and a tide-operated hydro-electric scheme. Apparently local residents were not at all unhappy when the scheme proved a nonstarter!

(Lef) The brickworks of Thomas Abell & Son at Withycombe as seen in the summer of 1929. The firm was responsible for building a number of local housing estates. Thomas Abell MBE JP figured prominently in the life of the town and served on the local Council for 54 years – from 1889 until his death in 1943.

(Below) Presumably a good time was had by all at this party, although some seem to have thought that you had to keep a straight face when posing for a photograph. It was said to have been organised to entertain children of unemployed local folk during the Depression of the 1930s.

(Opposite, top and middle) May 11, 1932 was a memorable day with the opening of the new Open Air Bathing Pool on the seafront. It cost £7,000 and proved a popular attraction for visitors and residents alike for around half a century. Before the pool was built, swimming galas and water-polo matches were played in the Dock basin against a backcloth of sheds, cranes and boats.

(Opposite, bottom) Employees of the Devon General Omnibus Company posed for a photographer outside the Company's offices and Depot in Imperial Road in the 1930s. They included three brothers – Charles, Fred and Henry Richards. Signs on the walls of the offices offered return day trips to Sidmouth and Seaton for 2/6d and 4/- respectively, while to go further, a day trip to the Doone Valley cost 9/6d.

Above we see the Ceremony of Crowning the May Queen at the Beacon School, round about 1932.

Below are the pupils in Standard 7 at the same school in 1933.They are Dorothy Pithers, Betty Bulling, Lucy Norman, Peggy Salter, Betty Robins, Eileen Tucker, Gladys Tooze, Joan Packer, Phyllis Horn and Peggy Dart.

Here we see a trophy-winning Exmouth soccer side, with club officials, in the 1933/ 34 season. And it seems that teams had mascots even in those days.

On Whit Monday 1936 the Urban District Council Chairman, J. J. Summers, officially opened the Phear Park Bowling Green and then posed with bowlers and spectators for a photograph. The first match on the new green then followed, in which Phear Park beat a team representing the Devon County Bowling Association Executive.

(Lef) The residents of Palace Cottages enjoy a street party to celebrate the Coronation of King George VI and Queen Elizabeth in 1937.

(Below) "Where is this 'birdie' I was told to watch?" is what the baby in the pram, Shirley Sansom (later to become Mrs Smale), seems to be thinking. The occasion was another Coronation party in Withycombe.

The town had its own Gas Company in 1937 with showrooms and demonstration rooms on the corner site of 21 Rolle Street. In the background is the area known as The Cross, a popular gathering place for residents on Saturday nights. It was badly damaged in an air raid in 1941.

On August 4, 1938 The Parade was awash. In those days this area was prone to flooding. Local resident Peggy Jago recalls being awakened early that morning by a heavy thunderstorm which led to the flooding and later watched people making their way to nearby Staples Buildings in rowing-boats. Among the properties affected was the shop run by her mother, Gladys Jago, in The Parade.

The equivalent of a modern-day pop-star attended an Exmouth festival on April 22, 1939. Elsie Carlisle (centre front) was well-known as a broadcaster and maker of gramophone records. This reception was held at Courtlands, home of Sir Garbutt Knott. He is in the picture along with the Director of the Imperial Institute; the Canadian Government Commissioner of Trade; Representatives of Governments in East Africa and Southern Rhodesia; and local councillors and officials, some with their wives.

In these days of mobile phones and many other wonders of communication, it is hard to realise that, for nearly half the century, all telephone calls had to be made through a switchboard operator at the local Exchange. On duty at the Exchange, above the former Post Office in Rolle Street, one day in May 1939, are telephonists Edna Bardens, Eileen Kenyon, Kathleen Helyer, Kathleen Stuart, Joyce Hocking, Edna Hardy and Ethel Boyland, watched by Exchange supervisor Miss Besley and the postmaster.

A unique record of Exmouth during the Second World War was kept by local resident Lena Ridge. In a small leather-bound note-book bearing the gold-lettered inscription "A note made now saves a wrinkled brow", Miss Ridge, of 43 Albion Street, recorded the date and time of every air-raid warning siren and every all-clear signal. She also in-cluded brief notes of particular incidents like "Salterton Road machine-gunned", "Plane brought down at B. Salterton" and "Bombs dropped at Parade, Exeter Rd; Phear Park, Strand Enclosure and Savoy". Lena Ridge's record shows that the siren was sounded 460 times in Exmouth and that 56 people were killed and 99 injured in raids on the town.

Patrolling the streets of Exmouth during the Second World War was the job of these war reserve policemen. Seen with Supt W. C. Johnson, Ins W. Abrahams and Sgt R. Lee are War Reserve Constables E. G. Manning; C. H. Avery; W. E. Ackland; R. H. Parker; R. J. Blewett; R. B. Bradford; S. Rees; S. H. West and L. G. G. Langdon.

This line-up of sergeants were all volunteers in the local Home Guard during World War II. Bill Gorfin (fourth from left, centre row) was one of the town's best-known characters through his work as journalist and editor of the *Exmouth Journal* for over half a century. His proud claim was of being the first local man to enrol in the Local Defence Volunteers, as the Home Guard was first known when set up in 1940. Others pictured include G. Seldon, T. Matthews, W. Croft, J. Pover, W. Pascoe, H. Lawes, F. Rendle, C. Tindall, W. Holman, J. Brock, W. Clarke, W. Bryant, R. Dixon, F. Troulan, R. Fairchild, R. Haydon, W. Pope, P. Maclarin, C. Havill, F. Havill, A. Pollard and C. Axon.

More of Exmouth's own "Dad's Army". Members of the local Home Guard Battery, Royal Artillery on September 24, 1944, prior to standing down after their wartime service. They include Capt Jones; 2/Lts Glanville and Southon; Sgts Walburn, Burnhill, Swinnerton and Raven; Bdrs Clode, Lowton and Bond; L/Bdrs Smith, Denford and Searle; and Gunners Andrews, Bolt, Doddrell, Fasey, Long, Skinner, Richards, Martin, Farrant, Pemberton, Steer, Gatter, Luxon, Thomas, Hitchcock, Thorn, Morrish, Edwards, Derrick, Hyde, Seager, Dudley, Eley, Heard, Pannell, Western, Williams, Stowell, Slocombe, Brailey, McIntosh, Harrish, Nicol and Sedgemore.

"Put that light out!" was a phrase very familiar to these members of the ARP or Civil Defence in World War II. Among the 16 air-raid wardens who posed for photographer Eric Castle in the grounds of All Saints Church were Messrs F. Copp, "Suzy" Wills, Fairchild, Fudge and Harry Stocker.

The same photographer used the same venue for this picture of another branch of wartime Civil Defence. Members of what was described as the "Civil Defence Mobile Gas Service", they included L. H. Bastin; J. A. Nelson; Mrs V. Mellish; Miss A. Spink; Mrs I. E. Bacon; Mrs M. T. Macmillan; C. A. Shute; G. H. Croft; Mrs K. R. Basgleppo; W. H. Cox; F. R. Matthews; Lt Col E. Clayton; H. W. Bastin; E. F. Bastin; W. German and Mrs I. F. Gale. Although the unit was fortunately never required to go into action, members had to report to its depot at the old Exeter Road Infants School each Thursday for training sessions and also every time an air-raid warning sounded. With one exception, the women members were all employed by day at the old Steam Laundry.

(Top and middle) Here are two pictures taken at a Second World War money-raising event, probably a Wings For Victory Week judging by the backcloth.

After the children taking part in a concert in New North Road, organised by Mrs Pidgeon, had been photographed, it was the audience's turn to face the camera. Among the young performers were Trevor Hynard, Geoff Murch, Mervyn Nicholas, Beryl Frost, Pam Vardy, Queenie Avery, Eileen Edds, Douglas Street, Betty Skinner, Pearl Willatt, Rita Avery, Majorie Skinner, Sheila Davey, Barbara Kettle, Pat Jarvis and Arthur Pidgeon.

(Below) VE Day and the end of the War in Europe in May 1945 saw much celebration and many street parties in the town, including this one in Union Street.

(Above) A boat has taken to the streets. No, not because of flooding but as part of a Carnival procession. Some sea-cadets in a cutter pulled by a lorry pass from The Strand into The Parade. They were members of the Sea Cadet Corps T. S. (Exmouth) Unit 395.

(Below) On parade on The Parade. Members of the Girls Life Brigade come to a halt outside the former Methodist Church. Among those on parade were Josephine Bonner, Jean Davey, Marion Evens, Betty Hawthorn, Pat Kelly, Jean Lewis, Margaret Shepherd, Rosemary Shepherd, and Doreen Strawbridge. Services were held at The Parade Methodist Church for 117 years until 1961. The original Woolworths shop may be seen in the background.

For many years swimming galas, including water-polo matches, attracted large crowds to the seafront pool on Saturday nights. Exmouth was noted for having strong water-polo teams and this junior team proved particularly successful in 1952.

Among the new schools to open in the district during the century was Marpool School in Moorfield Road. Pupils started to attend on September 4, 1952 and an official opening ceremony took place nearly three months later on November 24. Among the pupils celebrating the opening of their new school were Michael 'Buster' Williams, Tommy Williams, Peter Davidge, John Davidge, Ian Wilson, Gail Brown, Zena Bradford, Geoff Clarbull, Bill Pym, Tony Somers and John Hodge.

Crowds turned out on September 1, 1954 to watch the launching of the town's new lifeboat, *Maria Noble*.

Members of Exmouth Motor Club assemble at their meeting point in Hamilton Road sometime in the 1950s. Those present include Alan and Ivy Young, Trevor Hynard, Gerald Dommett, Clive Coate, Tim Wilson, Janet Hellier and Peter Stuart.

A familiar figure in Exmouth both before and after the Second World War was Mr A. E. ("Bert") Humphries. In November 1956, as chairman of the Urban District Council, he was in the Strand Gardens to receive an Olympic-style torch and a message of goodwill from the Mayor of Exeter. They had been carried from the city by a relay team of runners to inaugurate a Week of Prayer and World Fellowship of the YCMA. The final runner in the torch-bearing relay team, Greville Payne from Barbados, was accompanied on the final stretch from Courtlands Cross by three Exmouth runners – Maurice Southwell, Anthony Ellis and Trevor Free.

As might be expected in a seaside town, angling has always been a popular sport, with

an active local Sea Angling Club. On June 24, 1957, Mr Tom Sheppard (wearing cap and holding plaque) celebrated a victory in the company of fellow club members Messrs Addshead, Preston, Tony Hellier, Jack Freeman, Monat Walburn, Jim Shinn, Archie Sandcraft, Lionel Pulman and Stan Langdon. And if you are wondering, the dog was named Andy and belonged to Mr Freeman.

Harvest 1955, and pupils of Exeter Road Junior School pose around a table bearing the produce they have brought to school in thanksgiving.

Didn't they do well? On a cold night in the 1950s, these young St John Ambulance Brigade members won first prize in one section of the annual Carnival. Sue West (later Mrs Knight), seated extreme right, remembers how the scantily-dressed girls were given hot water bottles, to sit on or cuddle, to keep them warm. The float was built by Donald Madge and Bob Evans.

(Above) All the familiar characters are here: Mary, Joseph, Angels, Shepherds, Wise Men and a few extras besides. This Nativity play, produced by Mrs Esme Jones, was performed at Tower Street Methodist Church in the 1950s. Those taking part included Marylin Carnell, Anne Jones, Linda Davey, Michael Fogarty, Gillian Godman, Susan Morris, Marion Skinner, Alan Combes, Ian Mortimore, Peter Radford, Maurice Thorn, Stephanie Creedy, Carol Willatt, Mary Thorn, Geraldine Priddis, Enid Crump, Margaret Dart and Briony Creedy.

(Right) Snow has not been a particularly common feature of Exmouth's weather during the century, so when some did arrive in the early 1950s, these lads made the most of it. Enjoying themselves are Rodney "Beau" Musgrove, Geoffrey Skinner, Jack Lott, Terry Phillips, David Lavis, George Skinner and a lad named Dempster.

(Below) On March 20, 1952, local councillors and officers went underground to inspect a reservoir in Salterton Road. In the party were R. T. Weller, H. S. Burrow, S. V. Sheriff, W. J. Whitsed, D. P. Johnson, F. A. Tribble, M. N. Manson, Dr L. G. Anderson, G. Purcell, J. H. Down, F. N. Beckhart, R. J. Cochrane, H. J. Finnis, E. R. Delderfield, Brig J. H. Cameron- Webb, Cmdr K. M. Fardell, Mrs Fardell, J. L. Venus, Mrs Cochrane, F. W. Davey and R. J. Humphries.

(Above) The Rainbow Café was the venue for this children's party in 1952. It was one of the parties organised annually by the local Working Men's Club and run by Devon General bus driver Bill Tratt.

(Left) A big day in 1953 for Jean Manning was when she was crowned that year's Exmouth Carnival Queen. The ceremony was carried out by British film actress Patricia Plunkett, while smiling attendant Doreen Strawbridge looked on.

(Below) The new Thomas Abell Reference Library was opened on June 30, 1955. A former school in Exeter Road had been converted into the Devon County Council Branch Library nine years earlier. Prior to that there had been various libraries in the town, the most popular being one run by Exmouth Book Club at Manchester House. Those present at the Reference Library's official opening included Council chairman H. J. Finnis, George Abell, a descendant of Thomas Abell, and branch librarian Norman Chalk.

For most of the century, the Docks played a major part in the life of the town. Bill Peters, seen above (centre) with other employees of the Dock & Pier Company, was dockmaster for twelve years. He died in 1953 shortly after his retirement.

Below we see shoppers looking for a bargain at Walton's Departmental Store in November 1954. Situated on a corner site in Rolle Street, it was a favourite shopping venue and many folk still have happy childhood memories of visiting its Fairyland at Christmas. The store was destroyed by fire in January 1941, but a new building was eventually erected on the same site and trading continued there until 1989.

The hotel has gone, but its name lingers on. Dating from the days of the old coaching inns, the London Hotel occupied a prominent site in Chapel Street near its junction with The Parade. The hotel was demolished in the 1960s, but the memory of it continues with the nearby Council car park being called the London Inn Car Park.

Railway cuts made by Government Transport Minister Dr Beeching in the 1960s led to the loss of the branch line through Budleigh Salterton to Tipton St John. The station at Littleham, with its curved platform, disappeared and the cuts led to the number of platforms at the town's main station being reduced from four to the present-day one.